THE

COLLAPSE

OF A

GIANT

Donnie Melton

Published by Donnie Melton, 2010

This book is dedicated to all the hard-working Americans out there wondering what is going on with our country.

It is also for my daughter, Madyson, and every other young kid out there today, so that someday they will know that the history peddled in our classrooms today does not in fact depict the true stories behind our government and its leaders.

PREFACE

Like many of you, I have been watching events unfold on the news for the past several years and wondering what caused the terrible financial situation our country is in today. I have for the most part always considered myself a conservative-minded individual, but I also have always tried to consider the merits of both parties. When I heard of Mr. Bush starting these Wall Street bailouts back in 2008, I was enraged; a few years later, Mr. Obama's Health Care vote really sent me over the edge. I have now come to the conclusion that I am neither a Republican or a Democrat. This two-party system is flawed and full of nothing but life-long politicians with agendas. This book is about changing all of that. Our country is falling apart at the seams due to greed, bailouts, entitlements and the erosion of our beliefs in our creator. Our constitution has been trampled upon and our freedom is being challenged. We are in the middle of a battle for our way of life, not against terror regimes abroad, but against forces right here in our own country, elements of our government and our banks. As I do not wish to stay angry about these circumstances forever, I therefore decided to focus my righteous anger into the writing of this book. This book has been intentionally kept short and simple. I hope to touch on a select number of topics that should concern and unite the American people in a constructive way, in order to rage against the "Big Government" machine that has been slowly trying to make us dependent upon it. We will not be silent and stand aside while it goes about laying waste to our country. We do not aspire to be like other countries in the way we conduct policy – we are not other countries, we are the United States of America, empowered with rights given to us by our creator. May the Lord our God be with us in our fight.

TABLE OF CONTENTS

I

MONEY & GREED

Money is one thing that everyone must have in this day and age in order to survive. Unfortunately, at some point along our journey to the present we have come to believe that in order to obtain it we must seek it by the vilest means possible. Our society has reached the point where people will lie, cheat, steal, scheme, swindle, betray and even kill those closest to them in order to get it. In our modern culture, honesty and ethics have been tossed to the curb. This applies to not only individuals, but also organizations, cor-porations, and even our government. Of course, we can't control what every individual does, but shouldn't we at least have a say on how our government acts?

As a father and a mother model values for their children like honesty or personal restraint, so too should a government model certain basic values for its people in the way it conducts business. This should especially be true considering we are the ones writing the politicians' paychecks!

In this chapter, let's take a look at a few things that our giant government is doing. For example, let's consider how the lottery claims to put billions of dollars into our schools. What schools, and where are they located? If this *is* true, why are our schools so understaffed and our teachers so poorly paid? Here is one instance where billions of dollars seem to be totally unaccounted for, but oh well – let's move on!

While we're at it, let's talk about Social Security for a moment. I am 32 years old and have been working since the age of 17, but now they say that by the time I retire my benefits will be either drastically cut or not there at all. How is this possible? Fifteen years of paid taxes down the tubes, and that's just from one worker.

The problem with just being irritated about things like this is that we just let them go and in turn nothing gets done to fix the problem. The reason we let them go is that we think, "What can I do?" We feel powerless to make change happen. However, if enough people band together to make change, that is a much more pow-erful force to be reckoned with. I'll discuss the powerless thing in greater detail in Chapter 6. For now, let's move on.

I work a normal, full-time job and have done so for over fifteen years, paying my taxes just like everyone else does. However, in the springs of 2007 and 2009 I created a small company and a second job for myself. I was astonished to later find out that the tax rate for this activity is 33 1/3%. For example, if I make $10,000 working on this thing that *I* created, I have to pay the government $3,300 in taxes. Is this acceptable? Why is the government entitled to *so* much of my money? That $3,300 could have made a nice part-time income for someone else, but instead it just disappeared straight into the government's pocket. They do not extract, or for a better word *steal*, that much money from me at my regular job. Why am I being punished for my initiative?

What bothers me the most about this though is that even with all of this pickpocketing going on, our country is *still* in debt up to its eyeballs and *still* can't seem to make simple social programs work properly. We can't tax our way out of this problem, ladies and gentlemen – it is mathematically impossible. Yet our government continues to spend record amounts of money, insane sums that continue to push us further and further toward bankruptcy. Shouldn't our elected officials have to answer to the American people on how this money is being squandered? After all, we are the ones financing their spending! I resent the idea that after holding up my end of the bargain for fifteen years – paying my taxes like a decent, honest, law-abiding American – I am being told that my Social Security funds, and the Social Security funds of others my age, will either be greatly reduced or not even be there at all. It's not my fault that these officials have robbed Social Security money for other things so they can go on spending like drunken sailors. Why should I have to suffer the consequences? And you can be certain that if I ever failed to pay my taxes to the government, they would hold me accountable in a thousand ways; why can't I hold them accountable for wasting my hard-earned money on their pork barrel projects that benefit no one but themselves? This just enrages me, and I hope it enrages you too. We all have a right to be furious about this.

Here's my personal ideal solution on this issue, what I'd like to tell the government to do if I could: keep all of the Social Security money I have paid into the system for the past fifteen years – it's yours. Yeah, don't mention it. Just don't take any more from me! If you will do this one thing, I will gladly waive my retirement benefits. I could make far better use of my money by even just putting it in my local credit union at 1% interest.

Now, I know the above statement about 1% interest is going to drive those complex mathematicians in investor academia crazy because they're going to scream "Inflation!". I would like for them to prove to me that inflation outpaces government thieving and spending! However, if they're still worried about it, I have a simple solution for them: stop inflation!

What?

You see, I believe inflation is a man-made phenomenon caused by our Federal Reserve banking system (we'll talk more about our friends at the Fed in a later chapter). It's not just a given – we can control or even stop it. And it must be stopped – inflation is not only unnecessary, it's very destructive as well. Between inflation and taxation it's amazing that anyone can make any financial headway in this country.

Speaking of taxes, let's talk for a moment about various taxes and what they do for us. Let's start by listing some of the many random taxes imposed on us by the government. There is:

- Accounts receivable tax
- Building permit tax
- CDL tax
- Capital gains tax
- Corporate income tax
- Court fines
- Dog license tax
- Federal tax
- Federal unemployment tax (FUTA)
- Fishing license tax
- Food license tax
- Fuel permit tax
- Gas tax
- Hunting license tax
- IRS penalties (which are taxes
- Real estate tax
- Recreational vehicle tax
- Registration tax on your car
- Road toll tax
- Sales tax
- School tax
- Septic permit tax
- Social Security tax
- State tax
- State unemployment tax
- Telephone federal, state and local surcharge tax
- Telephone federal excise tax
- Telephone federal universal service fee tax
- Telephone minimum usage

- on top of tax)
- Inheritance tax
- Inventory tax
- Liquor tax
- Local income tax
- Luxury tax
- Marriage license tax
- Medicare tax
- Merchandise tax
- Military base factor adjustment tax
- Property tax
- surcharge tax
- Telephone recurring and non-recurring charges tax
- Tobacco tax
- Toll tunnel tax
- Utility tax
- Vehicle sales tax
- Watercraft registration tax
- Well permit tax
- Workers' compensation tax

Okay, still with me? Wow, I feel brain-dead from just inserting this list. The funny thing is, according to *goodcitizen.org,* a century ago *none* of these taxes existed, and our nation was *still* the most prosperous in the world, had absolutely *no* national debt, and had the *largest* middle class in the world (and Mom got to stay home to raise the kids!).

What the heck happened? I think we

can all agree based on even this cursory list of taxes that we are talking about an awful lot of money being taken in by our government. So how in the world are we at the point where not only is the government collecting *all of these taxes*, but also income tax and many other taxes not listed above, yet it's simply *not enough income*, and we therefore have to dig ourselves further into debt?

Our country is "by the people, for the people," right? Isn't that what Lincoln said? Isn't that what our government, our country, is supposed to be about? Well, I ask you – is this kind of behavior what we asked for? An ever-spiraling amount of taxation coupled with incredible amounts of government waste and an un-repayable national debt?

If we do not send a message to our government, nothing is ever going to change. At the end of this book there is a copy of our Constitution and our Bill of Rights. Dear reader, you may correct me if I am wrong (feel free to check), but I believe the Constitution states that any powers not given to the government revert back to the people. That means that together we have an awful lot of power. If you are as fed up with this crap as I am, let's begin to put these powers to use constructively and peaceably to make profound, well-defined positive change happen. Together we can send a message to our politicians that we will no longer be allowing their irresponsible spending sprees; from this day forward, their blank checks, written with the sweat of our brow, are cut off. Their license to spend our tax dollars on useless, money-pit programs has been revoked.

In terms of gathering together, the T.E.A. Party movement was a good start, but we must now work to organize it and put some direction behind it; no more just holding signs and holding rallies — let's hold these irresponsible men and women accountable! We must also refine the movement so that we can move beyond the petty name calling; we know we're right, so let's just plain-out prove them wrong through our deeds and our values. Leave the name-calling and the mud-slinging — the same old politics — to them. This must not be the same old politics under a different name — it must be a new movement of concerned, justified Americans from every walk of life working together to stop this insane federal spending and debt, *now.*

My friends, we must move to do this before it is too late; when 47% of Americans pay no taxes there is something very evil developing. Eventually, the 53% will grow weary of carrying the full country's burden.

I think we are now at the tipping point on the scale – things could easily go either way. Let's tip the scale back to a stable balance before our country starts to look too much like George Orwell's *1984.* When our country starts to look more like an Orwellian dystopia than the free land it should, we are heading into a scary point in history.

My family would love to go out and

spend a lot of money on whatever we want, but we live in the real world, with budgets and restraint.

So should our government.

II

THE MISSING LINK: MOM IN THE HOME

"Mom" is one of the most beautiful words in the world. Mom is the anchor of the home. Mom knows when her kids are sick, sad or happy, and how to love them in a way that is special.

In this day and age however, having Mom at home full-time has become difficult, and in some instances all but impossible, to pull off. You can see the effects of this shift in schools everywhere you look.

So why did she have to leave the house? First of all, let me say that I'm not suggesting that women shouldn't work if they choose to; women have every right to be in the workforce and are just as capable of performing jobs as men are. I'm simply pointing out that societal pressures coupled with high taxes and expenses have made it impossible for some women to make the decision to be a homemaker. And indeed, this is my argument as to why Mom had to leave her home and her children and enter the workforce: her family needed the income from two jobs, not just one, but besides, everyone was telling her that she needed to work in order to become "liberated" (I will focus on the causes of and the solutions to the former; the latter you should already realize is garbage to begin with).

Children need someone at home to keep abreast of their upbringing; I doubt many would argue that a child wouldn't benefit from having their mom at home with them, taking care of them and watching out for them. Having Mom in the home would give a child someone to keep tabs on who their friends are, how they are doing in school and in life – it would also give them someone to instill good values in them.

Unfortunately, as the world has changed in the last fifty to sixty years, there have become fewer and fewer stay-at-home moms. As a result, our children are growing up in ways they have never before. With both parents working and the internet easily accessible, they have the whole world at their fingertips. They are free to learn about anything and talk to anyone. Sure, it's a great big world out there, full of lots of interesting subjects and good people, but it is also full of many questionable subjects and not-so-good people.

The problem is that the majority of families have a hard time controlling these things because they are just too busy trying to eek out a living. Thinking back to when I was a kid of around 6 or 7 years old, I can remember very clearly how my grandparents' house functioned. It went something like this: on the weekends, all the kids and grand-kids came over to Grandpa and Grandma's house. The men fished, played horseshoes and relaxed in hammocks. The women played cards, laughed and cooked. The grand-kids played chase, perhaps went swimming depending on the season, and gathered blackberries for pies. Also, the grand-kids could gather their berries from the edge of anyone's land without worrying about being kidnapped, molested or encountering someone being angry or abusive. I can tell you for certain that I'm not imagining some fairy-tale utopia because I actually remember *doing* these things. Most people these days can't imagine letting their kids out of their sight for so much as a moment, much less letting them roam a mile or two away to pick berries or play with the neighbors' children. But, I digress. This was a beautiful time, even though every single man and woman worked hard during the week. On these days there was no one too tired to do things with the kids. We had family football and volleyball games. We all played croquet. We all spent time together, the kids and grand-kids had constructive fun while being watched by the adults, and no one had to worry about the children getting into trouble because they were being supervised.

Why was this all possible? First of all, things were cheap enough that one person could work and pay for a house, a car and basic living expenses and still have enough left over to pay for family recreation. It didn't hurt that the things people did for fun back then were a lot simpler and less expensive. Secondly though, and most importantly, Mom was at home and had time to keep up with the housework, cook meals and help the kids with their homework. Dad could eat, relax and get ready for the next day. Both parents had equally hard jobs, but they were both manageable. Mom held it all together.

Now journey from that era to the year 2010. Both parents come home completely exhausted and stressed to the max by the alarming rate of information transfer and cell phones ringing. Home but not really off, they try to figure out something quick to eat (which everyone usually eats in a different room while watching T.V.), then grab a shower and hop into bed to get up the next morning and do it all over again. By the time the weekend arrives everyone just wants to be left alone so they can rest a while before the vicious cycle starts anew on Monday. Forget spending the weekend having fun at Grandma and Grandpa's. Forget getting the housework done, or having a nice family meal, or getting the homework done, or even spending any meaningful time together. It's all everyone can do to survive another week without going insane; never mind having to deal with everything else.

Another source of trouble for kids today that results directly from this scenario is the lack of Mom's involvement in her kids' school and after-school lives. When I was a kid, no one was about to miss Family Saturday because they had to go to detention or SAC. This didn't happen because moms knew when their kids got in trouble at school, and they either dealt with it or told Daddy when he got home.

Either way, the situation was dealt with and the kid was corrected. In short, people were involved enough to give a crap.

These days it seems everyone is detached. Everyone is so busy from the day-to-day of just trying to survive financially that they have forgotten why it is so great to live in the first place. Where have we gone wrong when we need to work so hard to survive that we miss the most important times in our childrens' lives? Where have we gone wrong when we need to work so hard to survive that we are sacrificing the proper upbringing of our kids to do it?

Kids are growing up at a much faster rate now than they ever have before, both because of the increases in the speed of communication and increases in available knowledge. My wife has taught headstart and kindergarten, and now she teaches first grade; if you were to hear just half of what I have heard regarding goes on in schools today it would scare you to death. In our modern world it is apparently commonplace to encounter 5, 6 and 7-year-olds who hit teachers, curse and do other things that I do not even feel comfortable getting into here. There have been some days that my wife has come home and told me things that were so unfathomable that I could not properly respond for several minutes.

This is troubling to me, and it should be to you too. Of course, to make things even worse, most of the powers needed to deal with these things in a way that would actually be effective have been taken away from our teachers. In addition, prayer and the Pledge of Allegiance have been removed from our public schools, which only makes the atmosphere of these institutions worse.

Why have prayer and our country's pledge been removed? Certain minorities find these things offensive, that's why.

Well, let me tell you, that offends me, and it offends a lot of others who still believe in the true core values of this country! If I may digress for a moment, when and why did we start letting the minority rule the majority? Just because you don't believe in God doesn't mean everyone else should lose the right to exercise their beliefs. People of America, this has got to change! You know, with all of these atheists and Muslims complaining about "In God We Trust" being on our money, I wonder if they even realize what the other inscription on our money means. You know, "E Pluribus Unum"? It's Latin, and it means "out of many comes one". It's the idea that our country contains many different ethnicities, but was founded as one nation upon certain core, sacred religious principles that act to unite us and to make us whole.

If you don't want to be a part of that "one" then feel free to get the heck out of the country; I'm sure there are many people out there who would be more than willing to help you with your plane fare.

I realize that I've gone off on a bit of a tangent here, but I think it's important for us to stop and consider our core Christian values, and how alienating them by taking them out of the public sphere influences our children. Do we honestly want to keep allowing minorities to dictate our country's values, or do we want to stand up for the principles our nation was founded on?

Regarding Mom in the home: do we really need to keep taxes so high that both parents must work full-time in order to survive? Sure, cutting back on certain excessive luxuries could help, but at the end of the day lowering taxes would help immensely in relieving much of the burden America's families are feeling; in a lot of cases, it would be enough relief to allow Mom to stay home and raise her kids. That way she would be free to take care of her family, and to instill in her children important values and discipline.

President Ronald Reagan once said,

"All great change in America begins at the dinner table." Think of the positive change we could reap in America if Mom came back into our homes. We need Mom back, not to cook and clean and be a husband's servant, but to do the most difficult job of all in this country: raise the next generation of great American leaders.

Also, one final thing to keep in mind: I'll bet the Congressman or Senator's wife from your state at least has the *option* to stay at home, fully funded by your tax dollars. If she doesn't, it's not because of inflation or something like that; it's because she's spending too much money on the high-society lifestyle she enjoys, *also* courtesy of your tax dollars.

Not that she would ever actually risk running out of money; if she needed more, her husband would just vote himself and his cohorts a raise. They were probably planning to anyway. I bet that would be a through-and-through bipartisan initiative. Of course, they wouldn't have a problem telling you how the vote went on your next paycheck, under the taxes section – they've got to pay for their salaries somehow!

Dear reader, our only answer to the problems we face are prayer and action. Our 14th President, Franklin Pierce, once said that there is no national security without the acknowledgment of God. I will close this chapter with those wise words.

III

OUR LEADERS

English author Edward Bulwer-Lytton once wrote that the pen is mightier than the sword. As I start this chapter, I pray these words are true. Think of how long it has been since our nation has had a great visionary leader in office. Perhaps one might say we haven't had such a leader since Ronald Reagan. Some might go as far back as Thomas Jefferson. Certainly George Washington and Sam Adams come to mind, but have there been any such men since? I'm talking about men who had some integrity in their character, men who actually cared about the people and fought to make a positive difference for them.

One thing to note about these early great leaders is that when they were in office, campaign money was not something that necessarily gave them an edge over 99% of the country's population. Candidates today, although already wealthy beyond reasoning, are funded by what they refer to as "soft money", funds raised by special interest groups to help the individual in question be accepted as the nominee of either the Democratic or Republican party. Therefore, whoever eventually becomes elected already sold out while they were campaigning.

The early great leaders mentioned

above were admirable individuals who had solid ideals and deep character backed by a ton of resolve. What kind of people do we have running today? Men who cater to special interest groups and men who have deep pockets and are able to spend nearly limitless amounts of money to advance their cause. Everybody running these days makes promises they can't keep, pledging to use money that is not theirs to finance programs the American people do not want. (I know that some of you might view these statements as being partisan, but I feel it important to mention that I believe both parties in our two-party system are equally worthless).

Another thing: everyone says that you need to vote if you don't like what is going on in Washington, but how can voting really make a difference when in the presidential election the electoral college decides who wins? Who are these electoral delegates? Have you ever met one? I sure haven't. There have been numerous polls taken over the years about whether people would rather have the presidency decided by a popular vote or an electoral college. Depending on who you consult, as much as 78% of the American population wants to change the process to a popular vote (I wonder who the other 22% is?).

So, if three quarters of the American people want our system changed, why hasn't it been done? I like many other people feel that in presidential elections my vote doesn't even really count. With swing states and electoral delegates and all these other factors, what difference does my solitary vote make? And what guarantee do I have that my electoral delegate will even vote for the candidate he is supposed to be voting for? I have a horrible feeling that in many instances American citizens vote in vain for the candidates of their choice as the electoral college picks the Commander-in-Chief they feel will keep the money flowing in the directions they want it to flow in.

Now, moving forward, please do not misunderstand my position. I am a capitalist, and I'll fully support America as a capitalist society till my death. In the book *The Millionaire Next Door*, the authors present statistics to demonstrate that capitalism is the only form of society in which the little man even has a chance at becoming wealthy; according to them, eight out of ten millionaires in America are first generation wealthy – that is to say, they earned it themselves. This says to me that capitalism is one of the finest environments for people to live and work in because true capitalist societies are ripe with opportunity. However (and this is a very important distinction), there is a massive difference in my mind between your basic millionaire and your basic millionaire *politician*.

Basic millionaires (and let's be fair here: the word "basic" is fine when talking about millionaires because there are somewhere between 8 and 10 *million* millionaires worldwide depending on which statistics you cite) have worked hard to get to where they are and just want the government to stay out of their lives. On the other hand, basic millionaire *politicians* just want to control people. Once they control one thing they move right on over to the next. Before too long they will seek to control everything. This has led to some terrifying scenarios in our modern society. These kinds of individuals already have control of the banks, the bombs, the auto industry and now the insurance industry. Think about that for a moment — that's a huge amount of control over your life.

What right do these filthy rich politicians have to control these things, getting richer off the American people and seeking to put a tight leash on them? Government is an institution that by and large does not produce anything at all, and these politicians pulling the strings produce nothing either; they only consume.

My friends, we have got to place some people in office who will stand up for morality and who will have the integrity to truly listen to the will of the American people. We must do this soon, before we end up in a country we do not recognize. You see, when it comes to these millionaire politicians, control is not the only threat they pose; sure, they desire to make money off the hard work of the American taxpayers, but in their bids to stay in office, they also work to pacify minority special interest groups in order to raise money and gain re-election. This is dangerous for our country. You see, the leaders we have now are either agreeing with or standing idly by while people are having God removed from *everything* at an alarming rate:

Our courts are hearing insane requests from organizations like the A.C.L.U. to remove crosses at military cemeteries and war memorials.

Groups are pushing to have the Ten Commandments removed from courthouse property.

Atheists are filing lawsuits to forbid prayer groups in schools and public libraries.

I want you to understand, this is not an attack on atheists or Muslims as a whole; rather, it is an attack against the assault certain groups of these individuals are leading against our country's founding beliefs. We cannot be silent and simply watch while these groups seek to undermine our country's basic principles; we must act to stop them, before it's too late.

Proverbs 18:34 says, "Righteousness exalteth a nation, but sin is a reproach to any people". Our Lord also says that a man cannot serve two masters. So, we are either a God-fearing nation that upholds certain Christian values, or we are a people who cower down to minority views on religious subject matter. I pray we will be the former.

We need leaders in our elected offices who will step up and stand up for our value systems. If we do not find and elect such individuals to the offices of President and Vice President, and to the seats in our Congress and our Senate, our country is going to be laid waste to. If you don't think a thing like that could ever happen to a giant like America, perhaps you should read a book by David Wilkerson called *America's Last Call.* Mr. Wilkerson gives an exhaustive collection of Biblical references regarding civilizations that were destroyed throughout history because of their moral wickedness and idolatry. If it could happen to them, it can most certainly happen to us, and I am certain it will if we do not act soon.

My friends, when we place money and special interest groups in higher esteem than the Lord our God and basic moral values, we are most certainly heading for a fall. If we wish to avoid the wrath that is coming to us, we must work tirelessly to stop these individuals and groups who are tearing our country's values apart; once we have stopped them, we must then work tirelessly to restore the damage that has already been done. The restoration of our country will not be an easy task, but it is one worthy of the labor if we wish to leave anything pure and decent to our nation and our children after we pass on.

So, the big question is, in order to accomplish the task we must work toward, what would a good voting ballot look like for our future elections? I'm talking about the presidency all the way down to our congressmen. Since a fair portion of this book is based in my opinions, I'm going to give you my thoughts on what a dream ballot ticket would look like to me. Keep in mind, of course, that this is certainly not the only combination that would work, but just one possible roster that would "break the status quo," as our current smooth-talking President, Barack Obama, would phrase it:

For the Presidency I would nominate Ron Paul, and for the Vice Presidency I would nominate Chuck Swindoll.

Our Money Czar would be Dave Ramsey, and his answer to spending would be "no".

Our Senate seats would be filled by former military patriots, educators and people who have run successful small businesses.

The Congress seats would be filled by farmers, oil field workers and social workers.

No more *politicians* allowed.

By this point you are probably saying that this is crazy – how could these kinds of men and women run our country? Well, it's simple really: they help people through what they do every day. They know what real America is like, they know what real America means, and they know what real America needs. Who could ask for more in a representative?

Harry Truman once quipped that if you want a friend in Washington you should get a dog. Should our government really be this way? With a group of representatives like the ones I just mentioned, *everyone* would have a friend in Washington.

Let's talk for one moment about the characteristics of good leaders. First, we need people who fear the Lord our God. This should be first and foremost because the Bible says a fear of God is the beginning of true wisdom. Even if you have a different belief regarding religion I think we can agree that true wisdom would be a really beneficial characteristic for a representative to have in this day and age.

Secondly, our highest officials, our President and Vice President, should have some sort of common-sense money management skills. When I say this, I don't just mean some smart, smug lawyer. After all, a person can be smart and still lack common sense wisdom.

If we do not get genuine, moral representatives into our elected offices soon, the consequences could be dire; our failure to do so could very well lead to the collapse of our country. Loss of our freedoms also comes to mind as a consequence, but more on that in the next chapter. The point that I'm trying to underscore is that it is vital for us to work together to elect genuine leaders with character and virtue. It is one of the most important things we must do in order to repair the damage to our nation.

My hope is that we all speak up soon and try to make a difference. November is fast approaching. Edmund Burke once wrote that the only thing necessary for evil to prevail is for good men to do nothing. We The People, the common Americans – it is time for us to stand up and make a change that will rock this country to its very foundation. We must make a change that will return us to our founding principles and change the way we operate, change the way we treat people.

No more outrageous bailouts and

pork barrel projects for these loons in Washington financed by our money.

No more millionaire politicians trying to put a stranglehold on our freedoms.

No more special interest groups trying to tear down our values.

And to the politicians in Washington waiting anxiously for the elections coming in November, I have some words from Donald Trump to pass along to you:

"You're fired!"

IV

HEALTH CARE REFORM?

Caring for the sick who are not fortunate enough to have health insurance is something we are all concerned about. However, it is possible to do the right thing in the wrong way! If this statement wasn't true, people could do whatever they wanted in the name of good intentions and toss ethics out the window, because the results would all be the same. Of course, in the real world this is not the case; it is indeed very possible to try to do the right thing in the wrong way. Mr. Obama's Health Care reform bill is a perfect example of such an attempt.

In the beginning of Mr. Obama's bid to reform our health care system, I thought that his huge reform plan was supposed to be about health *insurance* reform. However, now that the legislation has evolved and finally passed, it is plain for me to see that it has turned into a series of government-sanctioned health care mandates.

Who are they to mandate us? We should be mandating them!

In the beginning our president talked to insurers and told them what he wanted done: no denials for pre-existing conditions, and no lifetime caps. These are both good things. However, after this meeting the insurance companies told Mr. Obama that they would do what he asked if he brought them a lot of new customers. Isn't this like bringing the pigeons to the cat, per se? Instead of standing up to the insurers and saying, "If you can't do what I request and in a fair way without gouging the American people, we will eliminate you and create something else", he buckled to their pressure and changed his position. Incidentally, what would "something else" look like? Well, we'll probably never know because this started during the bailouts. Too Big To Fail? That's just a bunch of crap! Entrepreneurs and small business owners would have been champing at the bit to solve our financial crisis and create other ways of banking, financing and insuring, but they were never given the chance. "Without struggle there can be no progress" comes to mind when thinking about Bear Sterns, Bank of America and A.I.G. Let them figure out their own problems! Regular Americans were not bailed out; instead they were punished by having to pick up the tab for these large corporations' failures through government takeovers. But, I digress – back to health care.

Let's think for a moment about how this health care bill puts into place over 17,000 new I.R.S. Agents, all of whom will be ready to step into your business to make sure you have health insurance that's up to government standards. Oh, that sounds really helpful. I don't know about you, but I've checked my tax records, and the last time I was given any help by the I.R.S. was way back in the year, uhm – oh, that's right! Never! Once these people get their greedy little hands in the cookie jar it's almost impossible to get them out! Are we seriously supposed to believe that adding 17,000 new money-grubbing bureaucrats to the equation here is going to be beneficial to *anyone*?

And let's consider what this plan does for our national debt. If you spend more money in one month than you actually have, this situation is called a "budget deficit". So, you borrow money and you go into "debt". Debt will cost you the amount borrowed plus interest. If you continue this cycle over and over again each month, eventually the interest payment on your loans will grow to be bigger than any individual item on your budget agenda.

Finally, when you get to the point where all of your money is going to the ever-expanding interest on your loan, and you have no money left over, you then become "bankrupt". Pretty simple, eh?

Well, each year since 1969, Congress has spent more money on various things than we the taxpayers have paid in. Whenever this happens, the Treasury Department has to borrow money to meet Congress' appropriations. Only now the Treasury Department is having problems finding lenders. What does this sound like to you? Nothing good, that's for sure.

Now, with all of this stupidity already going on, our politicians have enacted health care reform, which will be the largest tax ever in American history. How can we afford this? We can't.

When does it end? If your child misbehaved with money, would you open your wallet and give him or her more to use, thinking that he or she will *surely* do better this time, even without any corrective instruction or consequences for their initial misbehavior? Of course not! There must be some kind of consequence associated with misbehavior in order for someone (or a group of somebodies, in this case our government) to make changes.

Thomas Jefferson once said, "In questions of power, let us hear no more of trust in men, but bind them down from mischief with the chains of the Constitution". Well, we have got to bind these fanatics with *something*, because they sure as heck aren't abiding by the Constitution.

An acquaintance of mine at a manufacturing site who is in favor of this health reform legislation asked me recently if I had ever read anything by Thomas Sowell. I hadn't, yet. I think he meant to try to trip me up. However, I did do a little research later on Mr. Sowell, and here is what I found, Mr. Carter, under the notable quotes section at www.federalbudget.com: "For society as a whole, nothing comes as a right to which we are entitled. Even bare subsistence has to be produced... The only way anyone can have a right to something that has to be produced is to force someone else to produce it... The more things are provided as rights, the less the recipients have to work and the more the providers have to carry the load."

Wow, that's powerful stuff! Thanks,

Mr. Carter, for reinforcing my opinion on this crazy health care legislation. Even though you disagreed with me, you ended up helping me find a man with words of wisdom that everyone should hear!

Listen: we are all fast becoming slaves to entitlement programs and a national debt crisis. When the recent situation with the government bailouts started happening, I wasn't sure that in two terms of leadership our great country could be hurt enough to force our nation to go bankrupt. Unfortunately, as it turns out, I couldn't have been more wrong. I believe these politicians are going to pull it off if we don't move to stop them.

(Incidentally, let me just briefly note for the sake of bipartisan anger that Mr. Bush was the individual who first started these Wall Street bailouts, back in 2008)

Nancy Pelosi (and I'm paraphrasing here) said on March 21st, 2010 that our officials were making history with their vote on health care reform; she said they were joining the ranks of people who voted in favor of Social Security and Medicaid.

Am I the only one who sees that both of these programs were a bad idea, and that they're both on their way to bankruptcy while dragging the American people into collective bankruptcy in the process?

Of course, I have given a lot of criticism so far without a lot of suggestions about what could actually be done to improve the state of health care in this country. I am certain that there are things we could do to reform our health care system that would actually work very well and really help people, yet don't involve spending unreasonable sums of taxpayer money on ineffective programs. Unfortunately, the door for dialogue has already been slammed shut. So now, unless a new administration changes things back to the way they were, or the states that challenged the legality of this new legislation through lawsuits are successful in their efforts to get it overturned, the government and insurance companies will now wield absolute control over our medical welfare.

We have got to vote these control freaks out of office and come up with some real solutions, ones that will improve our health care system while not jeopardizing our freedom, ones that will increase accessibility while not passing a medical tab on to our children and grandchildren that will cause them to live in a far less fortunate society than the one we live in today.

Before I close, allow me to mention one other issue not directly related to the health insurance reform legislation that absolutely makes my blood boil: Allstate and their "Accident Forgiveness" commercials drive me insane. Accident forgiveness. Oh, so you'll forgive me? Forgive me for what? I pay for car insurance in case something *happens*, you condescending freakin' mongrels!

"But still, we won't raise your rates if you have an accident – you're welcome."

This is the insane kind of crap I'm talking about! The same kind of ridiculous things happen with health insurers: you pay and pay into the insurance company, and then when you have a heart attack you either get dropped or have your rates raised so high that you can't possibly afford to pay them. Of course, if you try to get insurance again, they'll bust you for having a pre-existing condition! These are all big problems, and they need real solutions. Sadly, instead of standing up to insurers and telling them that they are going to be bound by a code of ethics which would actually make them act like *human beings*, our leaders have opted to reward them by mandating that every American has to be one of their paying customers. How freaking unbelievable is that?

I will close this chapter with a plea to our elected officials and to the American people: please, do not let this happen in our country. If this legislation stands, soon the use of life support and the opportunity to be resuscitated will not even be options anymore, and a government-mandated health insurance company will weigh the value of you and your family's lives against a financial balance sheet, all in the name of "helping people". Baby boomers, this should really scare you, since you will soon be the biggest drain to a balance sheet in the near future. Makes you wonder if you were productive enough in your life, or paid enough taxes, to get a transplant of any organ you might need, doesn't it? They are giving these people control of our lives – we have to stop this.

We the people must stand and kill this legislation before it turns into a nightmare from which we cannot escape.

For those of you who think the fight ended with the vote – the fight isn't over until we lay down our challenges and surrender our liberties into the hands of government bureaucrats (who have never fixed anything).

Finally, I just could not bring myself to end this chapter without raising a question about the Patriot Act, as I believe it parallels this Health Care reform.

Without the people's consent our representatives made this law that invades our privacy in the name of the "greater good". Doesn't this infringe upon our most basic God-given rights, the right to be left alone and the right protecting against illegal search and seizure when, in the comfort of your own home, you cannot even have a private phone conversation?

Why was this not enacted in other points in history, like after the Oklahoma City Bombing or even Pearl Harbor? Because people would have went flippin' crazy, that's why! After September 11th, people were in such shock that our politicians got away with this outrageous legislation. Some elements of the bill could have been good, I suppose, but they took it a mile too far.

The cleverest way for our leaders to take our freedom and our country away from us would be without firing a single shot. Mr. Bush asked us to trust him about national security and look where it got us: to less freedom. Now Mr. Obama is doing the same thing, asking us to trust him with our health care system. Will we stand idly by and allow our leaders to control us like this? Will we be duped again? This is definitely something to think about, because one day we will have to explain these decisions we made to our children.

I want to be able to say to my daughter that, doing all I could, I tried to stand for freedom and the Lord our God, even if it flew in the face of political agendas.

What say you?

V

THE FEDERAL RESERVE

The beautiful thing about learning the truth is that it sets you free to know and not wonder.

It's not surprising to me that a lot of Americans are ignorant to the fact that the Federal Reserve is not actually federal, per se. A business friend of mine once said, "It is about as federal as Federal Express." *I* think the answer is that it lies somewhere in the middle. They report to Congress, but only to a certain extent. They are most definitely not transparent. Either way though, the Fed is one of the largest, most challenging problems we must face if we are going to fix what is wrong with America.

When I was a kid, we learned the Golden Rule, and it was as follows: do unto others as you would have others do unto you. In our post-moral society, however, this rule has been changed into: he who has the gold rules. In this case though, we are really talking about Federal Reserve notes, which is to say paper money.

This money is created by the Federal Reserve, with virtually no oversight, by high powered bankers and economists who are so egotistically presumptuous as to believe that they can arbitrarily decide what interest rates ought to be. This reckless minting of money without regards to its validity is what causes that nasty word "inflation".

Imagine if we were able to create money for ourselves and adjust our rates in the name of the "general good". We would have unlimited power. That is a scary thing, because it flies in the face of how the powers of government are defined by our Constitution. Think of the power such an organization could wield! For example, where is the money going that we passed out in TARP? The answer is that it is going to banks, who misbehaved in the first place causing all this mess. It is, of course, given to them by the Federal Reserve, some of whom are bankers themselves. This being said, lacking strict oversight by our officials, this conglomeration is the most powerful institution in the world.

Since Congress really did not in my opinion have the constitutional authority to create this institution, but does have the power to abolish it, why don't they? It only causes problems for Americans, generating issues like inflation that could otherwise be controlled. Yet our politicians refuse to act. The situation almost leads you to believe they are being paid off in some way, doesn't it?

Our president said recently that he wanted to reform our financial system so that there would never have be government bailouts of institutions "too big to fail" again. The problem with this is that the Federal Reserve itself was originally created to bail out institutions, in order to prevent another Great Depression from happening. When F.D.R. allowed this to happen he sold us out from a money-backed gold standard to a standard of money backed by absolutely nothing, thus opening the door for banks to misbehave and subsequently be bailed out by an unregulated Federal Reserve that just basically counterfeits money to make things look better than they actually are. We need to regulate our government to keep them from creating crazy, irresponsible institutions like the Federal Reserve that they can't even control.

Ronald Reagan once said, "Government is not the solution to the problem. Government is the problem". I could not agree more with this statement. The problem is that all of these politicians say these kinds of things and yet the government is now bigger than it ever has been, and they always talk about balancing our budget, but how in the world can you balance a budget when the institution that creates money out of thin air is setting interest rates and is virtually price-fixing goods, services and housing has no accountability? The people who created the problem cannot be objective enough to fix it, and we cannot expect to rely on their help.

The Federal Reserve needs to be audited. I suppose our course from there would depend on the results of that audit, but I can almost guarantee you that we would want to abolish the Fed if the truth about that institution was ever actually told. We have the legal authority to do this, to my understanding, if Congress doesn't possess the power; remember, any powers not awarded to the government by the Constitution revert to being the peoples. I truly believe this is something that we would want to do.

All the reading that I've done indicates to me that if we did away with the Federal Reserve, inflation in the sense that we know it would die. I also believe that with the Fed gone and our money returned to a gold or silver standard, the government and banks would have to sit down and actually count cost before spending. Imagine, accountability! This in turn would lower taxes because if our leaders were not allowed to spend us into oblivion (money doesn't just grow on trees anymore – it has to be backed by something!) they would not get to tax us into it. Under

Article 1, Section 8 of our constitution it calls for the Congress to set weights and balances on currency. What the heck are they waiting for?

Although this is one of my shortest chapters, it is second in importance only to a return to Godly Biblical principles, because without this huge change in monetary policy we will always have to live under the human golden rule as mentioned earlier instead of God's Golden Rule.

So, let's abolish this evil, non-transparent institution and return to a system of true weights and balances. To be able to accomplish this we cannot rely upon the same people who created the problem to fix it, save for a few genuine individuals like Ron Paul. For the most part, these people will not shoot themselves in the foot, so to say. Therefore, we need new God-fearing men to lead us in this endeavor – let's go find them!

By the way, if you don't believe me about this "legal" counterfeiting institution, I strongly suggest you read Congressman Ron Paul's book, *End the Fed*. You will not regret having educated yourself through reading this man's wisdom.

VI

A SUMMATION
ON THE
AMERICAN DREAM

As Americans living at this point in history, we stand facing the future, gazing down three possible paths we can travel.

These three paths could not be more different from one another. However, two of these three paths do have one thing in common. Although one is far to the right and the other is far to the left, neither one has led us in a truthful, God-fearing direction for a very long time. All that either of these paths have done for many years is fight with each other over control of our direction; as a result, they have caused us to lose our way. They both started out straight and narrow, but have become broad and crooked.

There were supposed to have been men of honor and restraint directing us down these paths, but along the way they sold us out for fortune and control. The men along these paths are now so ethically compromised that they no longer care if they lead men, women or even the next generation of children down the path toward a calamity beyond belief. The men on these pathways have done the un-imaginable: they have sold out the American people, and for what – money? For the love of money is the root of all evil.

They have given up our country's founding principles to satisfy ultra-rich bankers and insurance executives. They have created profits for oil companies in freedom's name, while spilling the blood of American soldiers.

We can't take back the harm these men have caused. All we *can* do is decide to travel in a new direction. Which leads us to the third path.

The third path is our opportunity to start over again and begin traveling in the right direction. Thank you, Lord, for your grace that is new every day. As we move forward this time, may we be reminded that it is you we want to follow; we need Your truth be our guide, not the almighty dollar.

We choose to follow hope. The two

party system we leave behind. We no longer accept the idea that an independent can't compete for office because they aren't allowed the interview time or can't afford to run.

We welcome new ideas based on sound principles.

As we travel this new path full of opportunity, we travel together: We The People have once again joined together to walk with our God and take responsibility for our own actions. Even if our progress is slow and our challenges difficult, we will keep our eyes fixed above, for we know where our strength comes from.

As we walk forward together, the men on the other paths will laugh at us, and mock us. They will tell us we can't do this. But as we grow in number and in strength, their laughs will slow and then finally stop. The men on those other paths will stop laughing because they will realize that when we unite together, moving forward as one in the name of our freedoms and our principles, we cannot be stopped. They will see then that their days of power and influence are numbered, and they will be afraid. A large group of like-minded Americans working as one toward a common goal is a hard thing to stop; with the Lord as our guide, we cannot and will not be stopped.

For many years the men on the other paths have been trampling our rights. For many years they have been recklessly spending our money and curbing our freedoms. As a result, the process of taking back our country will most likely take much time. This is not something that we are good at as Americans – patience. In this instance however, we must strive to be ever patient, working slowly but surely to rebuild our shattered nation while taking every opportunity to make positive change when the chance presents itself. It will take much time and much patience, but I know that in the end we will stay true to the third path, and over the course of time we will prove ourselves to be the victors.

We will show these Washington bureaucrats that in the short term they may have taken some things away from us, but in the end we will get them back, and that they will never take them away again. Anything that is imposed upon a man without his consent, beyond the basic laws to which societies abide, is the equivalent of communism. We do not consent, and we will abide these things no longer.

Will you choose to walk with me down the third path? It is definitely not the easiest one to travel. In order to travel this path, a man has to look at himself in the mirror every morning and realize that he is accountable for his own actions. Will you be accountable for your own actions? Will you come with us?

We should not rely on the government for our solutions. We *are* the solutions. America has some of the best and brightest minds in the world today. We do not need to be taken care of by people who can't even balance a budget – we can take care of ourselves. Millions of families across America balance their budget every month. It only requires two things to do so:

restraint, and discipline. These things our politicians lack, and so we choose to leave them behind.

We are a hard-working, good-hearted people, full of resolve. Our resolve is currently being tested, and I'm afraid we are going to have to show them that we have no limit to how long we will endure in order to protect our freedoms. But we have no limit, and we will show them.

Dear friend, if you are still reading this book that tells me that you agree with at least some of what I'm saying. Even if we disagree on some things, that's alright. It's the beauty of being free humans – we can each follow our own beliefs.

Let us be united. Our message is simple but of grave importance: no more politics and no more deception. This is the people's country, and you would do well to listen, for we are taking it back.

Remember, the only necessary for evil to prevail is for good men to do nothing.

VII

U.S. CONSTITUTION
&
BILL OF RIGHTS

i. Constitution

We the People of the United States, in Order to form a more perfect Union, establish Justice, insure domestic Tranquility, provide for the common defence, promote the general Welfare, and secure the Blessings of Liberty to ourselves and our Posterity, do ordain and establish this Constitution for the United States of America.

Article I

Section 1. All legislative Powers herein granted shall be vested in a Congress of the United States, which shall consist of a Senate and House of Representatives.

Section 2. The House of Representatives shall be composed of Members chosen every second Year by the People of the several States, and the Electors in each State shall have the Qualifications requisite for Electors of the most numerous Branch of the State Legislature.

No Person shall be a Representative who shall not have attained to the age of twenty five Years, and been seven Years a Citizen of the United States, and who shall not, when elected, be an Inhabitant of that

State in which he shall be chosen.

Representatives and direct Taxes shall be apportioned among the several States which may be included within this Union, according to their respective Numbers, which shall be determined by adding to the whole Number of free Persons, including those bound to Service for a Term of Years, and excluding Indians not taxed, three fifths of all other Persons. The actual Enumeration shall be made within three Years after the first Meeting of the Congress of the United States, and within every subsequent Term of ten Years, in such Manner as they shall by Law direct. The Number of Representatives shall not exceed one for every thirty Thousand, but each State shall have at Least one Representative; and until such enumeration shall be made, the State of New Hampshire shall be entitled to chuse three, Massachusetts eight, Rhode-Island and Providence Plantations one, Connecticut five, New-York six, New Jersey four, Pennsylvania eight, Delaware one, Maryland six, Virginia ten, North Carolina five, South Carolina five, and Georgia three.

When vacancies happen in the Representation from any State, the Executive Authority thereof shall issue Writs of Election to fill such Vacancies.

The House of Representatives shall chuse their Speaker and other Officers; and shall have the sole Power of Impeachment.

Section 3. The Senate of the United States shall be composed of two Senators from each State, chosen by the Legislature thereof, for six Years; and each Senator shall have one Vote.

Immediately after they shall be assembled in Consequence of the first Election, they shall be divided as equally as may be into three Classes. The Seats of the Senators of the first Class shall be vacated at the Expiration of the second Year, of the second Class at the Expiration of the fourth Year, and the third Class at the Expiration of the sixth Year, so that one third may be chosen every second Year; and if Vacancies happen by Resignation, or otherwise, during the Recess of the Legislature of any State, the Executive thereof may make temporary Appointments until the next Meeting of the Legislature, which shall then fill such

Vacancies.

No Person shall be a Senator who shall not have attained to the Age of thirty Years, and been nine Years a Citizen of the United States and who shall not, when elected, be an Inhabitant of that State for which he shall be chosen.

The Vice President of the United States shall be President of the Senate, but shall have no Vote, unless they be equally divided.

The Senate shall chuse their other Officers, and also a President pro tempore, in the Absence of the Vice President, or when he shall exercise the Office of President of the United States.

The Senate shall have the sole Power to try all Impeachments. When sitting for that Purpose, they shall be on Oath or

Affirmation. When the President of the United States is tried, the Chief Justice shall preside: And no Person shall be convicted without the Concurrence of two thirds of the Members present.

Judgment in Cases of Impeachment shall not extend further than to removal from Office, and disqualification to hold and enjoy any Office of Honor, Trust or Profit under the United States: but the Party convicted shall nevertheless be liable and subject to Indictment, Trial, Judgment and Punishment, according to Law.

Section 4. The Times, Places and Manner of holding Elections for Senators and Representatives, shall be prescribed in each State by the Legislature thereof; but the Congress may at any time by Law make or alter such Regulations, except as to the Places of chusing Senators.

The Congress shall assemble at least once in every Year, and such Meeting shall be on the first Monday in December, unless they shall by Law appoint a different Day.

Section 5. Each House shall be the Judge of the Elections, Returns and Qualifications of its own Members, and a Majority of each shall constitute a Quorum to do Business; but a smaller Number may adjourn from day to day, and may be authorized to compel the Attendance of absent Members, in such Manner, and under such Penalties as each House may provide.

Each House may determine the Rules of its Proceedings, punish its Members for disorderly Behaviour, and, with the Concurrence of two thirds, expel a

Member.

Each House shall keep a Journal of its Proceedings, and from time to time publish the same, excepting such Parts as may in their Judgment require Secrecy; and the Yeas and Nays of the Members of either House on any question shall, at the Desire of one fifth of those Present, be entered on the Journal.

Neither House, during the Session of Congress, shall, without the Consent of the other, adjourn for more than three days, nor to any other Place than that in which the two Houses shall be sitting.

Section 6. The Senators and Representatives shall receive a Compensation for their Services, to be ascertained by Law, and paid out of the Treasury of the United States. They shall in all Cases, except Treason, Felony and Breach of the Peace, be privileged from Arrest during their Attendance at the Session of their respective Houses, and in going to and returning from the same; and for any Speech or Debate in either House, they shall not be questioned in any other Place.

No Senator or Representative shall, during the Time for which he was elected, be appointed to any civil Office under the Authority of the United States, which shall have been created, or the Emoluments whereof shall have been encreased during such time: and no Person holding any Office under the United States, shall be a Member of either House during his Continuance in Office.

Section 7. All Bills for raising

Revenue shall originate in the House of Representatives; but the Senate may propose or concur with Amendments as on other Bills.

Every Bill which shall have passed the House of Representatives and the Senate, shall, before it become a Law, be presented to the President of the United States; if he approve he shall sign it, but if not he shall return it, with his Objections to that House in which it shall have originated, who shall enter the Objections at large on their Journal, and proceed to reconsider it. If after such Reconsideration two thirds of that House shall agree to pass the Bill, it shall be sent, together with the Objections, to the other House, by which it shall likewise be reconsidered, and if approved by two thirds of that

House, it shall become a Law. But in all such Cases the Votes of both Houses shall be determined by Yeas and Nays, and the Names of the Persons voting for and against the Bill shall be entered on the Journal of each House respectively. If any Bill shall not be returned by the President within ten Days (Sundays excepted) after it shall have been presented to him, the Same shall be a Law, in like Manner as if he had signed it, unless the Congress by their Adjournment prevent its Return, in which Case it shall not be a Law.

Every Order, Resolution, or Vote to which the Concurrence of the Senate and House of Representatives may be necessary (except on a question of Adjournment) shall be presented to the President of the United States; and before the Same shall take Effect, shall be approved by him, or being disapproved by him, shall be repassed by two thirds of the Senate and House of Representatives, according to the Rules and Limitations prescribed in the Case of a Bill.

Section 8. The Congress shall have Power To lay and collect Taxes, Duties, Imposts and Excises, to pay the Debts and provide for the common Defence and general Welfare of the United States; but all Duties, Imposts and Excises shall be uniform throughout the United States;

To borrow Money on the credit of the United States;

To regulate Commerce with foreign Nations, and among the several States, and with the Indian Tribes;

To establish an uniform Rule of

Naturalization, and uniform Laws on the subject of Bankruptcies throughout the United States;

To coin Money, regulate the Value thereof, and of foreign Coin, and fix the Standard of Weights and Measures;

To provide for the Punishment of counterfeiting the Securities and current Coin of the United States;

To establish Post Offices and post Roads;

To promote the Progress of Science and useful Arts, by securing for limited Times to Authors and Inventors the exclusive Right to their respective Writings and Discoveries;

To constitute Tribunals inferior to the supreme Court;

To define and punish Piracies and

Felonies committed on the high Seas, and Offences against the Law of Nations;

To declare War, grant Letters of Marque and Reprisal, and make Rules concerning Captures on Land and Water;

To raise and support Armies, but no Appropriation of Money to that Use shall be for a longer Term than two Years;

To provide and maintain a Navy;

To make Rules for the Government and Regulation of the land and naval Forces;

To provide for calling forth the Militia to execute the Laws of the Union, suppress Insurrections and repel Invasions;

To provide for organizing, arming, and disciplining, the Militia, and for governing such Part of them as may be employed in the Service of the United

States, reserving to the States respectively, the Appointment of the Officers, and the Authority of training the Militia according to the discipline prescribed by Congress;

To exercise exclusive Legislation in all Cases whatsoever, over such District (not exceeding ten Miles square) as may, by Cession of particular States, and the Acceptance of Congress, become the Seat of the Government of the United States, and to exercise like Authority over all Places purchased by the Consent of the Legislature of the State in which the Same shall be, for the Erection of Forts, Magazines, Arsenals, dock-Yards, and other needful Buildings;--And

To make all Laws which shall be necessary and proper for carrying into Execution the foregoing Powers, and all other Powers vested by this Constitution in the Government of the United States, or in any Department or Officer thereof.

Section 9. The Migration or Importation of such Persons as any of the States now existing shall think proper to admit, shall not be prohibited by the Congress prior to the Year one thousand eight hundred and eight, but a Tax or duty may be imposed on such Importation, not exceeding ten dollars for each Person.

The Privilege of the Writ of Habeas Corpus shall not be suspended, unless when in Cases of Rebellion or Invasion the public Safety may require it.

No Bill of Attainder or ex post facto Law shall be passed.

No Capitation, or other direct, Tax shall be laid, unless in Proportion to the

Census or Enumeration herein before directed to be taken.

No Tax or Duty shall be laid on Articles exported from any State.

No Preference shall be given by any Regulation of Commerce or Revenue to the Ports of one State over those of another: nor shall Vessels bound to, or from, one State, be obliged to enter, clear or pay Duties in another.

No Money shall be drawn from the Treasury, but in Consequence of Appropriations made by Law; and a regular Statement and Account of Receipts and Expenditures of all public Money shall be published from time to time.

No Title of Nobility shall be granted by the United States: And no Person holding any Office of Profit or Trust under them, shall, without the Consent of the Congress, accept of any present, Emolument, Office, or Title, of any kind whatever, from any King, Prince, or foreign State.

Section 10. No State shall enter into any Treaty, Alliance, or Confederation; grant Letters of Marque and Reprisal; coin Money; emit Bills of Credit; make any Thing but gold and silver Coin a Tender in Payment of Debts; pass any Bill of Attainder, ex post facto Law, or Law impairing the Obligation of Contracts, or grant any Title of Nobility.

No State shall, without the Consent of the Congress, lay any Imposts or Duties on Imports or Exports, except what may be absolutely necessary for executing it's inspection Laws: and the net Produce of all

Duties and Imposts, laid by any State on Imports or Exports, shall be for the Use of the Treasury of the United States; and all such Laws shall be subject to the Revision and Controul of the Congress.

No State shall, without the Consent of Congress, lay any Duty of Tonnage, keep Troops, or Ships of War in time of Peace, enter into any Agreement or Compact with another State, or with a foreign Power, or engage in War, unless actually invaded, or in such imminent Danger as will not admit of delay.

Article II

Section 1. The executive Power shall be vested in a President of the United States of America. He shall hold his Office during the Term of four Years, and, together with the Vice President, chosen for the same Term, be elected, as follows:

Each State shall appoint, in such Manner as the Legislature thereof may direct, a Number of Electors, equal to the whole Number of Senators and Representatives to which the State may be entitled in the Congress: but no Senator or Representative, or Person holding an Office of Trust or Profit under the United States, shall be appointed an Elector.

The Electors shall meet in their respective States, and vote by Ballot for two Persons, of whom one at least shall not be an Inhabitant of the same State with themselves. And they shall make a List of all the Persons voted for, and of the Number of Votes for each; which List they shall sign and certify, and transmit sealed to the Seat of the Government of the

United States, directed to the President of the Senate. The President of the Senate shall, in the Presence of the Senate and House of Representatives, open all the Certificates, and the Votes shall then be counted. The Person having the greatest Number of Votes shall be the President, if such Number be a Majority of the whole Number of Electors appointed; and if there be more than one who have such Majority, and have an equal Number of Votes, then the House of Representatives shall immediately chuse by Ballot one of them for President; and if no Person have a Majority, then from the five highest on the List the said House shall in like Manner chuse the President. But in chusing the President, the Votes shall be taken by States, the Representation from each State having one Vote; A quorum for this Purpose shall consist of a Member or Members from two thirds of the States, and a Majority of all the States shall be necessary to a Choice. In every Case, after the Choice of the President, the Person having the greatest Number of Votes of the Electors shall be the Vice President. But if there should remain two or more who have equal Votes, the Senate shall chuse from them by Ballot the Vice President.

The Congress may determine the Time of chusing the Electors, and the Day on which they shall give their Votes; which Day shall be the same throughout the United States.

No Person except a natural born Citizen, or a Citizen of the United States, at the time of the Adoption of this

Constitution, shall be eligible to the Office of President; neither shall any Person be eligible to that Office who shall not have attained to the Age of thirty five Years, and been fourteen Years a Resident within the United States.

In Case of the Removal of the President from Office, or of his Death, Resignation, or Inability to discharge the Powers and Duties of the said Office, the Same shall devolve on the Vice President, and the Congress may by Law provide for the Case of Removal, Death, Resignation or Inability, both of the President and Vice President, declaring what Officer shall then act as President, and such Officer shall act accordingly, until the Disability be removed, or a President shall be elected.

The President shall, at stated Times,

receive for his Services, a Compensation, which shall neither be encreased nor diminished during the Period for which he shall have been elected, and he shall not receive within that Period any other Emolument from the United States, or any of them.

Before he enter on the Execution of his Office, he shall take the following Oath or Affirmation:--"I do solemnly swear (or affirm) that I will faithfully execute the Office of President of the United States, and will to the best of my Ability, preserve, protect and defend the Constitution of the United States."

Section 2. The President shall be Commander in Chief of the Army and Navy of the United States, and of the Militia of the several States, when called into the actual Service of the United States; he may require the Opinion, in writing, of the principal Officer in each of the executive Departments, upon any Subject relating to the Duties of their respective Offices, and he shall have Power to grant Reprieves and Pardons for Offences against the United States, except in Cases of Impeachment.

He shall have Power, by and with the Advice and Consent of the Senate, to make Treaties, provided two thirds of the Senators present concur; and he shall nominate, and by and with the Advice and Consent of the Senate, shall appoint Ambassadors, other public Ministers and Consuls, Judges of the supreme Court, and all other Officers of the United States, whose Appointments are not herein otherwise provided for, and which shall be established by Law: but the Congress may by Law vest the Appointment of such inferior Officers, as they think proper, in the President alone, in the Courts of Law, or in the Heads of Departments.

The President shall have Power to fill up all Vacancies that may happen during the Recess of the Senate, by granting Commissions which shall expire at the End of their next Session.

Section 3. He shall from time to time give to the Congress Information of the State of the Union, and recommend to their Consideration such Measures as he shall judge necessary and expedient; he may, on extraordinary Occasions, convene both Houses, or either of them, and in Case of Disagreement between them, with

Respect to the Time of Adjournment, he may adjourn them to such Time as he shall think proper; he shall receive Ambassadors and other public Ministers; he shall take Care that the Laws be faithfully executed, and shall Commission all the Officers of the United States.

Section 4. The President, Vice President and all civil Officers of the United States, shall be removed from Office on Impeachment for, and Conviction of, Treason, Bribery, or other high Crimes and Misdemeanors.

Article III

Section 1. The judicial Power of the United States, shall be vested in one supreme Court, and in such inferior Courts as the Congress may from time to time ordain and establish. The Judges, both of the supreme and inferior Courts, shall hold their Offices during good Behaviour, and shall, at stated Times, receive for their Services, a Compensation, which shall not be diminished during their Continuance in Office.

Section 2. The judicial Power shall extend to all Cases, in Law and Equity, arising under this Constitution, the Laws of the United States, and Treaties made, or which shall be made, under their Authority;--to all Cases affecting Ambassadors, other public Ministers and Consuls;--to all Cases of admiralty and maritime Jurisdiction;--to Controversies to which the United States shall be a Party;--to Controversies between two or more States;--between a State and Citizens of another State;--between Citizens of different States;--between Citizens of the same State claiming Lands under Grants of different States, and between a State, or the Citizens thereof, and foreign States, Citizens or Subjects.

In all Cases affecting Ambassadors, other public Ministers and Consuls, and those in which a State shall be Party, the supreme Court shall have original Jurisdiction. In all the other Cases before mentioned, the supreme Court shall have appellate Jurisdiction, both as to Law and Fact, with such Exceptions, and under such Regulations as the Congress shall make.

The Trial of all Crimes, except in Cases of Impeachment, shall be by Jury; and such Trial shall be held in the State where the said Crimes shall have been committed; but when not committed within any State, the Trial shall be at such Place or Places as the Congress may by Law have directed.

Section 3. Treason against the United States, shall consist only in levying War against them, or in adhering to their Enemies, giving them Aid and Comfort. No Person shall be convicted of Treason unless on the Testimony of two Witnesses to the same overt Act, or on Confession in open Court.

The Congress shall have Power to declare the Punishment of Treason, but no Attainder of Treason shall work Corruption of Blood, or Forfeiture except during the Life of the Person attainted.

Article IV

Section 1. Full Faith and Credit shall

be given in each State to the public Acts, Records, and judicial Proceedings of every other State. And the Congress may by general Laws prescribe the Manner in which such Acts, Records, and Proceedings shall be proved, and the Effect thereof.

Section 2. The Citizens of each State shall be entitled to all Privileges and Immunities of Citizens in the several States.

A Person charged in any State with Treason, Felony, or other Crime, who shall flee from Justice, and be found in another State, shall on Demand of the executive Authority of the State from which he fled, be delivered up, to be removed to the State having Jurisdiction of the Crime.

No Person held to Service or Labour in one State, under the Laws thereof, escaping into another, shall, in Consequence of any Law or Regulation therein, be discharged from such Service or Labour, but shall be delivered up on Claim of the Party to whom such Service or Labour may be due.

Section 3. New States may be admitted by the Congress into this Union; but no new States shall be formed or erected within the Jurisdiction of any other State; nor any State be formed by the Junction of two or more States, or Parts of States, without the Consent of the Legislatures of the States concerned as well as of the Congress.

The Congress shall have Power to dispose of and make all needful Rules and Regulations respecting the Territory or other Property belonging to the United

States; and nothing in this Constitution shall be so construed as to Prejudice any Claims of the United States, or of any particular State.

Section 4. The United States shall guarantee to every State in this Union a Republican Form of Government, and shall protect each of them against Invasion; and on Application of the Legislature, or of the Executive (when the Legislature cannot be convened) against domestic Violence.

Article V

The Congress, whenever two thirds of both Houses shall deem it necessary, shall propose Amendments to this Constitution, or, on the Application of the Legislatures of two thirds of the several States, shall call a Convention for proposing Amendments, which, in either Case, shall be valid to all

Intents and Purposes, as Part of this Constitution, when ratified by the Legislatures of three fourths of the several States, or by Conventions in three fourths thereof, as the one or the other Mode of Ratification may be proposed by the Congress; Provided that no Amendment which may be made prior to the Year One thousand eight hundred and eight shall in any Manner affect the first and fourth Clauses in the Ninth Section of the first Article; and that no State, without its Consent, shall be deprived of its equal Suffrage in the Senate.

Article VI

All Debts contracted and Engagements entered into, before the Adoption of this Constitution, shall be as valid against the United States under this

Constitution, as under the Confederation.

This Constitution, and the Laws of the United States which shall be made in Pursuance thereof; and all Treaties made, or which shall be made, under the Authority of the United States, shall be the supreme Law of the Land; and the Judges in every State shall be bound thereby, any Thing in the Constitution or Laws of any State to the Contrary notwith-standing.

The Senators and Representatives before mentioned, and the Members of the several State Legislatures, and all executive and judicial Officers, both of the United States and of the several States, shall be bound by Oath or Affirmation, to support this Constitution; but no religious Test shall ever be required as a Qualification to any Office or public Trust under the United States.

Article VII

The Ratification of the Conventions of nine States, shall be sufficient for the Establishment of this Constitution between the States so ratifying the Same.

Done in Convention by the Unanimous Consent of the States present the Seventeenth Day of September in the Year of our Lord one thousand seven hundred and Eighty seven and of the Independence of the United States of America the Twelfth

In witness whereof We have hereunto subscribed our Names,

George Washington--President and deputy from Virginia

New Hampshire: John Langdon, Nicholas Gilman

Massachusetts: Nathaniel Gorham, Rufus King

Connecticut: William Samuel Johnson, Roger Sherman

New York: Alexander Hamilton

New Jersey: William Livingston, David Brearly, William Paterson, Jonathan Dayton

Pennsylvania: Benjamin Franklin, Thomas Mifflin, Robert Morris, George Clymer, Thomas FitzSimons, Jared Ingersoll, James Wilson, Gouverneur Morris

Delaware: George Read, Gunning Bedford, Jr., John Dickinson, Richard Bassett, Jacob Broom

Maryland: James McHenry, Daniel of Saint Thomas Jenifer, Daniel Carroll

Virginia: John Blair, James Madison,

Jr.

North Carolina: William Blount, Richard Dobbs Spaight, Hugh Williamson

South Carolina: John Rutledge, Charles Cotesworth Pinckney, Charles Pinckney, Pierce Butler

Georgia: William Few, Abraham Baldwin

ii. Bill of Rights

Article I

After the first enumeration required by the first article of the Constitution, there shall be one representative for every thirty thousand, until the number shall amount to one hundred, after which the proportion shall be so regulated by

Congress, that there shall be not less than one hundred representatives, nor less than one representative for every forty thousand persons, until the number of representatives shall amount to two hundred; after which the proportion shall be so regulated by Congress, that there shall be not less than two hundred representatives, nor more than one representative for every fifty thousand persons.

Article II

No law varying the compensation for the services of the Senators and Representatives, shall take effect, until an election of Representatives shall have intervened.

Article III

Congress shall make no law

respecting an establishment of religion, or prohibiting the free exercise thereof; or abridging the freedom of speech, or of the press; or the right of the people peaceably to assemble, and to petition the Government for a redress of grievances.

Article IV

A well regulated Militia, being necessary to the security of a free State, the right of the people to keep and bear Arms, shall not be infringed.

Article V

No Soldier shall, in time of peace be quartered in any house, without the consent of the Owner, nor in time of war, but in a manner to be prescribed by law.

Article VI

The right of the people to be secure in their persons, houses, papers, and effects, against unreasonable searches and seizures, shall not be violated, and no Warrants shall issue, but upon probable cause, supported by Oath or affirmation, and particularly describing the place to be searched, and the persons or things to be seized.

Article VII

No person shall be held to answer for a capital, or otherwise infamous crime, unless on a presentment or indictment of a Grand Jury, except in cases arising in the land or naval forces, or in the Militia, when in actual service in time of War or public danger; nor shall any person be subject for the same offence to be twice put in jeopardy of life or limb; nor shall be compelled in any criminal case to be a witness against himself, nor be deprived of life, liberty, or property, without due process of law; nor shall private property be taken for public use, without just compensation.

Article VIII

In all criminal prosecutions, the accused shall enjoy the right to a speedy and public trial, by an impartial jury of the State and district wherein the crime shall have been committed, which district shall have been previously ascertained by law, and to be informed of the nature and cause of the accusation; to be confronted with the witnesses against him; to have compulsory process for obtaining witnesses in his favor, and to have the Assistance of Counsel for his defence.

Article IX

In Suits at common law, where the

value in controversy shall exceed twenty dollars, the right of trial by jury shall be preserved, and no fact tried by a jury, shall be otherwise re-examined in any Court of the United States, than according to the rules of the common law.

Article X

Excessive bail shall not be required, nor excessive fines imposed, nor cruel and unusual punishments inflicted.

Article XI

The enumeration in the Constitution, of certain rights, shall not be construed to deny or disparage others retained by the people.

Article XII

The powers not delegated to the United States by the Constitution, nor prohibited by it to the States, are reserved to the States respectively, or to the people.